ABCs
in Nature

Daniel Nunn

Chicago, Illinois

www.capstonepub.com
Visit our website to find out more information about Heinemann-Raintree books.

To order:

☎ Phone 800-747-4992

💻 Visit www.capstonepub.com to browse our catalog and order online.

Edited by Dan Nunn and Rebecca Rissman
Designed by Joanna Hinton-Malivoire
Picture research by Ruth Blair
Originated by Capstone Global Library Ltd
Production by Alison Parsons

Library of Congress Cataloging-in-Publication Data
Nunn, Daniel.
ABCs in nature / Daniel Nunn.
p. cm.—(Everyday alphabet)
ISBN 978-1-4109-4732-1—ISBN 978-1-4109-4737-6 (pbk.) 1. English language–Alphabet–Juvenile literature. 2. Nature–Juvenile literature. I. Title.
PE1155.N87 2012
428.13—dc23   2011043716

Acknowledgments
We would like to thank the following for permission to reproduce photographs: iStockphoto p. 26 (© Viorika Prikhodko); Shutterstock pp. 4 (© Geanina Bechea), 5 (© nokhoog_buchachon), 6 (© EcoPrint), 7 (© Zurijeta), 8 (© D&D Photos), 9 (© Steve McWilliam), 10 (© Paul McKinnon), 11 (© Noam Armonn), 12 (© Sari Oneal), 13 (© Mariusz S. Jurgielewicz), 14 (© DUSAN ZIDAR), 15 (© Yellowj), 16 (© Zinaida), 17 (© Jill Battaglia), 18 (© mlorenz), 19 (© SAMBLAS Frederic), 20 (© nikonfotogger), 21 (© Pichugin Dmitry), 22 (© Scorpp), 23 (© Astronoman), 24 (© Mariephotos), 25 (© ventdusud), 27 (© Andrew Williams), 28 (© Malgorzata Kistryn), 29 (© Dmussman), 30 (© Serg64, © 12qwerty), 31 (© Africa Studio, © Sebastian Knight, © Photoseeker).

Cover photograph of a field of flowers and a tree reproduced with permission of Shutterstock (© Aleksandr Stennikov).

Every effort has been made to contact copyright holders of any material reproduced in this book. Any omissions will be rectified in subsequent printings if notice is given to the publisher.

Contents

Aa

acorn

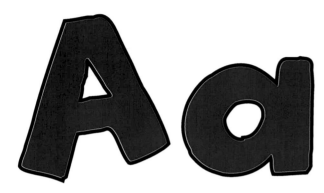

Acorns grow on oak trees. An acorn has a seed inside. One day this tiny seed might grow into a giant oak tree.

4

B b

butterfly

A butterfly is a type of insect. Many butterflies have beautiful patterns on their wings.

Cc
crab

Crabs live on the seashore. Most crabs walk sideways!

Dd

daisy

A daisy is a pretty yellow and white flower.

7

Ee

eggs

Birds lay eggs. The eggs hatch into baby birds.

8

Ff
frog

Frogs are happy on land and in water. They are also very good at jumping!

Gg

geese

Geese are a type of bird. A group of geese is called a "gaggle."

Hh

honey

Honey is made by bees. The bees make the honey in their hives or nests.

Ii

icicles

An icicle is a long, thin spike of ice. It is very cold to touch!

Jj

jellyfish

Jellyfish live in the sea.
Never touch a jellyfish.
It might sting you.

13

Kk
kitten

A kitten is a baby cat. Most kittens have blue eyes. The color changes when the cat gets older.

Ll

ladybug

A ladybug is a type of beetle. Many ladybugs are red with black spots. Some are other colors.

15

M m

moon

The moon is in the sky. You can see it best at night. This is a full moon.

Nn

nest

A nest is a home built by a bird or animal. Many birds build their nests in trees.

owl

There are many different types of owls. This is a saw-whet owl.

Pp

pigeons

A pigeon is a type of bird. People once used pigeons to deliver messages!

Qq

quack

What do ducks say? Why, "quack," of course!

Rr

rainbow

Rainbows happen when sunlight shines on drops of rain in the sky.

Ss

seashell

You can find empty seashells at the beach. Each seashell used to be part of a different sea creature.

Tt

tail

Lots of animals have a tail. Many animals use their tail to help them keep their balance.

23

Uu

udder

Female cows, sheep, and goats have udders. They use them to give milk.

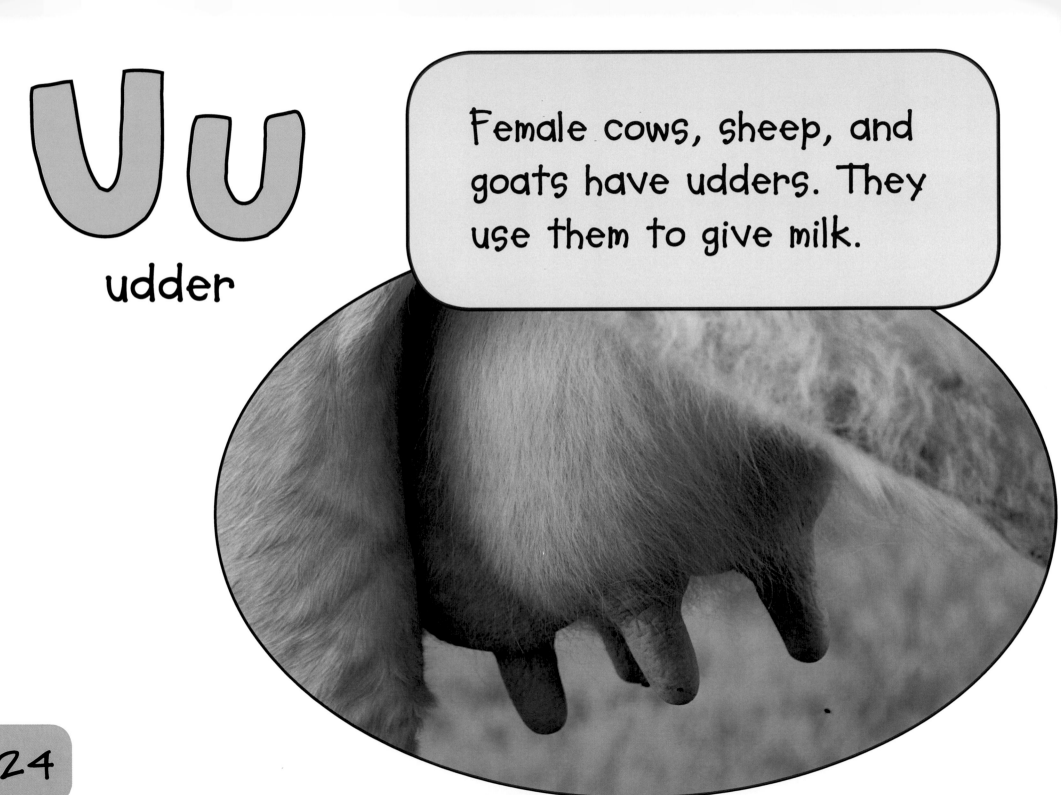

Vv

vegetables

Vegetables are plants that people eat. Vegetables are good for you!

25

Ww

worms

Earthworms live in soil. There are many other types of worms, too.

Xx

x-ray fish

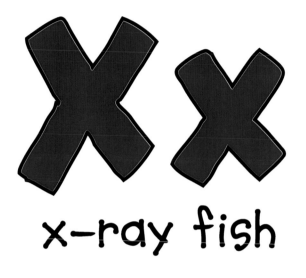

An x-ray fish is a funny color. You can see through part of its body!

yellow

Yellow is a color.
Sunflowers are yellow.
Can you think of any
other yellow flowers?

Zz

zebras

A zebra is an animal from Africa. It looks like a horse with black and white stripes!

Find Your Own ABCs in Nature

Can you find your own ABCs in nature? How many different things beginning with each letter can you find? Here are some ideas to help you!

Cc

Ff

Index